SINGAPORE

EXOTIC ASIA SERIES

SINGAPORE

"*my* new colony thrives most rapidly," wrote Stamford Raffles in 1819, shortly after he founded Singapore. "This is by far the most important station in the East; and as far as naval superiority and commercial interests are concerned, of much higher value than whole continents of territory."

At the time it seemed like an outlandish statement — a young English nabob comparing a sparsely populated, malaria-infested island with India and other established parts of the British Empire. But in retrospect, nearly two centuries later, we can forgive Raffles' unabashed enthusiasm because Singapore has grown into every thing he envisioned and more.

Singapore is now one of the world's largest ports, with hundreds of ships at anchor at any given time. It has one of the world's busiest and most efficient airports, a model to aviation experts around the globe. It has developed into one of Asia's most important manufacturing, trading and banking centres. And the three million Singaporeans enjoy one of the earth's highest standards of living, having made the ambitious jump from third to first world in recent years.

Singapore is also a model of social symmetry. Raffles split his nascent city into distinct neighbourhoods because he believed that different religious and ethnic groups should be segregated. But modern Singapore is a paragon of racial and theological tolerance, a country where Chinese, Malays, Indians and Eurasians live in harmony, forging a nation built around the principles of hard work, sacrifice and family values.

Singapore has always been a magnet for people who want to experience the energy and enchantment of Asia's great crossroads, a city that never quits, an island that blends eastern exoticism with western efficiency. And many of the most esteemed visitors have been writers, the literary lions of the British Empire — Conrad, Kipling, Coward and Maugham — for whom the island was a source of both inspiration and succour.

Rudyard Kipling was amazed by Singapore's bustling waterfront: "Providence conducted me along a beach in full view of five miles of shipping — five solid miles of masts and funnels!" Somerset Maugham was more interested in the human aspects, especially British colonial society: "The English in their topees and white ducks, speeding past in motor-cars or at leisure in their rickshaws, wear a nonchalant and careless air."

Despite the dozens of literary tributes, Singapore still has an astounding ability to surprise, perhaps because it rarely lives up to the abundant rumours and preconceived notions. There are, in fact, two very different Singapores — like "chalk and cheese" as the colonial Brits used to say — stark opposites that you would never expect to find within the same urban confines. Yet they easily mingle, weaving in and out like a Hindu dancer, a different face with every movement, earthly pleasures around every curve, veiled in a thin shroud of silk.

Many visitors pack their bags with visions of incense and orchids, and that's exactly what they find in Singapore's ethnic enclaves, where life seems to have changed little since the days of the British

Raj. Great swaths of Chinatown, Little India and Kampong Glam have been spared the wrecking ball, preserving the essential soul of Singapore, or more a constellation of souls, because each neighbourhood is a tiny nation unto itself.

Souvenir shops have overtaken much of Chinatown, but you can still hear the metallic clamour of the rickshaw workshops and visit dank temples where bananas and joss sticks are placed before gunnysack clad gods. Little India is more a feast for the eyes and nose, a flash of silk *saris* and scarlet turbans that swirls around a scent of saffron, curry and flowers, like a part of Bombay that's somehow drifted into the middle of a modern Western city. Kampong Glam and Arab Street are at their best at Ramadan, when the area erupts in a late-night frenzy of blinking lights and succulent food stalls where Muslims break their daily fast.

Singapore swarms with religious celebrations too, from a sedate Easter Sunday service in a whitewashed colonial church like Saint Andrew's Cathedral, to a wild and crazy Chinese event called the Monkey God's Birthday during which Taoist mystics are taken over by simian spirits, to the annual Thaipusam Festival in which Hindu devotees puncture their lips, cheeks and eyelids with metal skewers as an act of pious self-flagellation.

The old neighbourhoods also offer an easy introduction into ethnic eating, the delectable cuisines of China, India and the Malay archipelago. Outdoor eating areas called "hawker stalls" are something

of a local institution, places where locals flock for the
best chicken rice, *satay*, fish-head curry, *roti prata* and other
tasty meals. But Singapore has grown increasingly "cultured"
in recent years with cosmopolitan restaurants that feature
foods from around the world — French, Italian, American
and even Mexican. Many of the best eating places are
in hotels, but historic conservation areas like Tanjong Pagar,
Boat Quay and Emerald Hill are also magnets for upmarket cuisine.

Modern Singapore couldn't be more different, a cyberpunk vision of some future cosmos with gleaming
steel-and-glass towers and meticulous underground trains, a place where microchips have taken over from
manpower and where robots do much of the work once reserved for coolies. Modern Singapore works
better — and harder — than just about any city in the world.

Singapore wouldn't be what it is today without the blood, sweat and tears of human labour. Indian
convict workers who built the roads, buildings and the vast port. Chinese coolies who humped hundred-
pound loads of coal, coconuts and other commodities. Robust rickshaw boys who pulled their European
masters between home and office. And stout washerwomen who pounded clothes along the banks of
the Singapore River.

But now the island marches to the beat of a different drummer: the buzz, grind and whirl of automation.
Sophisticated robots finish concrete and operate pile drivers at construction sights. Longshoremen have
turned over their toughest tasks to huge cranes, computers and the other machines that run the modern

container port. Don't expect to find women pounding clothes on the river banks, because Singapore has one of the world's highest per capita rates of washing machine ownership. There are still a few elderly rickshaw boys around, but that's just tourist stuff, superseded by cars, buses and an ultra-efficient subway system that hums just below the surface.

Progress of this sort has made its mark on many Asian cities. But what makes Singapore different is an absolute obsession with automa-tion — an aspiration to become the world's most high-tech nation by early in the next century.

Nearly everywhere you go in Singapore you can see the results of this love affair with machines. There is a computer for every 12 people — the world's seventh highest per capita figure. Government, finance, transport, industry, social services and education are linked by a complex system of computer networks. And the Mass Rapid Transit (MRT) system is a model of high-tech efficiency, with computers that keep constant tabs on everything from the air conditioning and lighting, to statistics on the number of passengers and their commuting habits.

Automation has also worked its way into the tourist industry. Haw Par Villa (the old Tiger Balm Gardens) bills itself as the world's first high-tech Chinese mythological theme park, with lasers, audio-visual shows, and a sage robot — dressed like an old man — who spins tales of ancient myth and legend. Robots also play a part in Clarke Quay, a refurbished historical area along the Singapore River which features an automated journey through local history.

Yet behind the facade of office towers and shopping malls, Singapore is still a tropical island at heart. In fact, a third of the land area is still given over to forests, parks and gardens.

Bukit Timah is the grandfather of the island's nature reserves, set aside in 1883 as a patch of pristine rainforest and significant today because it's the only Singapore forest that has never been logged. Beneath a canopy of towering trees, the jungle trails are dark at midday. From the crest of Bukit Timah hill — Singapore's highest point — you can gaze out across the massive undeveloped heart of the island, a primeval panorama of misty rainforest and blue-grey lakes.

What Singapore hasn't been able to preserve, it has been able to recreate within the confines of the world famous Botanic Gardens on Tanglin Road, one of the best places to stroll or jog in Singapore. The collection of plants, flowers and trees is unmatched in Southeast Asia, especially the marvellous orchid enclosure. Much of the park is manicured to perfection, but there's also a large tract of virgin rainforest with indigenous tropical trees. Another leader in its field is the Singapore Zoological Gardens. Started after World War Two as a menagerie of cast-off British military pets, the zoo has grown into a dazzling wildlife showcase that combines education and entertainment. The zoo features animals from around the globe, but its forte is Southeast Asian fauna, including the world's largest colony of orangutans.

So despite its tiny size — the smallest nation in Asia — Singapore offers an incredible diversity of historical, cultural and organic attractions, an island where nearly all of Asia comes together in one place.

a *bove*:
Singapore's national
flowers are exported
all over the world
from the Mandai
Orchid Farm.
Although very few
orchids are native
to the island,
commercial
cultivation was
pioneered in
Singapore by John
Laycock, who
developed the first
strain that had a
long enough
lifespan to stand
up to the rigours of
overseas export.
right: Golf is taken
very seriously in
Singapore, which
boasts some of
Asia's best private
and public courses
like the picturesque
seaside links on
Sentosa Island.
opposite: The Botanic
Gardens offer a
peaceful haven
away from the
scurry of the city.
Founded in 1859,
the gardens display
more than 2,500
varieties of plants
and flowers.

eft: Singapore's parks and gardens take on many forms, like the immaculately landscaped Chinese Garden with its Sung Dynasty-style pagodas and 65-metre ornamental bridge. *above*: Emerald Hill Conservation District has some of the best examples of restored Peranakan shophouses, once derelict buildings but now much sought-after homes. Peranakan architecture is a synthesis of Indian, Malay, Chinese and British colonial styles.

left: Orchard Road may be synonymous with shopping in the daytime, but at night, Singapore's youth party here at the multitude of clubs, discos, karaoke rooms, bars and open-air cafes. The distinctive building with the pagoda-shaped roof is the Dynasty Hotel. *right*: On the bank of the Singapore River, recently restored Boat Quay offers a plethora of restaurants and bars with a choice of al fresco romance or air-conditioned comfort.

*t*he colourful Chingay Parade hits Orchard Road and other downtown streets on the fourth day of Chinese New Year. You don't have to be Chinese to participate: Singaporeans of all races and creeds join the celebration, an extravaganza of sight, sound and motion.

left: The most enduring symbol of Singapore's colonial past, Raffles Hotel reopened its doors in 1991 after a massive, three-year restoration programme. Many of the world's most famous writers have stayed at Raffles including Somerset Maugham, Joseph Conrad, Rudyard Kipling, Noel Coward, Hermann Hesse and James Michener. *right*: Singapore Slings are available at the Long Bar in Raffles, true to the original 1915 recipe. The hotel also features a museum with memorabilia of the famous people who have slept there.

*l*eft: A Nonya (Straits Chinese lady) dons a traditional wedding dress at the Peranakan Place Museum on Orchard Road. *above*: Empress Place Museum features a revolving display of treasures from the best museums in mainland China, like this exhibition of artifacts from the Silk Road. The handsomely restored structure also features an Asian art gallery, Chinese restaurant and souvenir stores.

a *bove*: Chinese opera is still very popular in Singapore, especially at festival times, when impromptu "wayang" stages are erected in neighbourhood parks and outside temples. *right*: During the annual Chingay Parade stilt walkers, Chinese opera stars and floats cavort to the dramatic sounds of crashing cymbals and pulsating drums. *opposite*: Fukkienese string puppets in Chinatown, one of Singapore's fading arts.

*l*eft: It's said that Singaporeans live to eat. Local sustenance includes (clockwise from upper left) Malay satay with peanut sauce, Indian curry and Chinese chicken rice. Other culinary influences derive from Indonesia, Portugal and Britain. *above*: The popular Satay Club opposite the Padang specializes in succulent roast meats on skewers eaten with raw onions, cucumber, sticky rice and a tangy peanut sauce.

a *bove*: Once the home of wealthy Arab traders, Alkaff Mansion in Telok Blangah Park has been restored into one of Singapore's finest restaurants, with succulent Asian food served in an elegant ambience. *right*: Lau Pa Sat Festival Market (formally called Telok Ayer) was originally constructed in Glasgow and shipped to Singapore in 1894. Several years ago its octagonal caste-iron frame was dismantled to avoid damage during the construction of the nearby subway station. Recently reassembled, the market now offers drinks, food, entertainment and shops.

a *bove*: Behind
colonial Raffles
Hotel towers the
massive Raffles City
complex, emblem-
atic of modern
Singapore and its
high tech profile.

right: The National
Museum started life
as a storehouse for
Sir Stamford
Raffles' natural
history and
anthropology
collections. Today
the museum
specializes in the
art, history and
culture of Asia.

*P*revious pages: There's fast and furious action during the International Dragon Boat Festival, staged in late May or early June on the calm waters of Marina Bay. *left*: Characters from the "Journey to the East" at Haw Par Villa/Dragon World, which bills itself as the world's first high-tech Chinese mythological theme park. *right*: One of Haw Par Villa's most endearing symbols is the Laughing Buddha, one of the hundreds of plaster figures left over from the days when the park was called Tiger Balm Gardens.

*l*eft: An elderly resident of Chinatown watches the busy ebb and flow of people along her street; much of the old neighbourhood is currently being restored, the hundred-year-old shophouses fitted out with modern plumbing, electricity and other conveniences. *above*: A trishaw driver takes a break in a Chinatown alley; Singapore once had thousands of trishaw and rickshaw "boys" but their number has dwindled to a handful in modern times.

left: Tanjong Pagar Restoration Area is set against a backdrop of Shenton Way and the downtown financial district. Shophouses in Tanjong Pagar have been transformed into stylish offices, antique shops, restaurants, bars and traditional Chinese teahouses. *above*: Scattered around Singapore are pockets of historic buildings, like this block of Peranakan shophouses along Koon Seng Road that have been gazetted by the government for conservation and restoration rather than demolition.

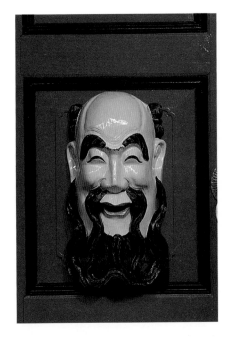

*O*pposite: For some prized songbirds, Sunday mornings mean an outing with their owners to the Wah Heng Coffee House in Tiong Bahru to show off their warbling skills. *above*: A calligrapher displays his handiwork, red scrolls with hand-written messages that are said to bring luck, wealth, harmony and health to anyone who hangs them at home. Some messages can be bought "off the rack" while others are made to order. *left*: A traditional Chinese mask finds a new use as a door knocker for an Emerald Hill shop.

l *eft*: Trishaws like this one in Little India still ply the streets of Singapore, mainly catering to the tourist trade, but some locals still use them for short hops. *right*: Of all the tropical fruits available in Singapore, the most loved — and hated — is the durian. The controversy lies in the durian's potent flavour and pungent aroma.

a *bove:* Orangutans greet visitors at the Singapore Zoological Gardens. One of the world's best zoos, the park specializes in rare and endangered Southeast Asian animals. It's latest feature is a unique night zoo, the only one of its kind in the world. *right:* Jurong Bird Park is a refuge for endangered species of the feathered kind — like these Caninde Macaws — and also a wonderful place to discover more about tropical birds and plants.

l *eft*: Underwater World on Sentosa Island has a moving walkway to guide you through 80 metres of acrylic tunnel, providing close-up views of a Pacific Ocean habitat with multi-coloured tropical fish and more dangerous species like sharks and rays. *above*: You can reach Sentosa Island — Singapore's largest theme park — by a breathtaking cable car ride from the mainland, then use the monorail to visit various attractions like the Pioneers of Singapore history exhibit, a live butterfly enclosure, the rare stone museum, an Asian arts and crafts village, and Underwater World.

a bird's eye view of Singapore's Financial District and Marina Bay By the middle of the next century the bay will be surrounded by lofty structures as the downtown area expands onto reclaimed land.

*a*bove: Mr Teo Ban Kok, the itinerant maskmaker of Chinatown, hawks his splendid papier-mache wares from an overloaded cart. *right*: Traditional dragon dance. The dragon symbolizes benevolence, strength and masculine force in the universe and is present at all Chinese festivals and most other important occasions. *opposite*: Sri Mariamman temple in Chinatown is the oldest and most important Hindu shrine in Singapore and is dedicated to Mariamman, one of the nine forms of the mother goddess Devi. The Thimiti firewalking festival is held here in September or October each year.

*O*pposite: Vesak Day celebrations honour Lord Buddha's birthday, including rituals designed to cleanse negative deeds from your past. These devotees are praying in the main hall at Phor Kar See Temple in Bright Hill. *above*: Before land reclamation, Thian Hok Keng Temple in Chinatown was situated on the Singapore waterfront. Sailors and their families used to flock here asking for safe journeys, offering prayers to Machu-po, goddess of the sea. *left*: Chinese temple architecture at Bright Hill.

*l*eft: The Sultan Mosque in Kampong Glam comes alive during Hari Raya, the joyous celebration after Ramadan. The month of Ramadan is marked by penitence and abstinence while Hari Raya is a time for forgiveness, feasting and family reunion. *right*: A resident of Little India holds an oil lamp during the colourful Deepavali Festival.

l *eft*: The imposing Sentosa Island Ferry Terminal also houses shops, restaurants and a monorail station. *right*: The Merlion, a mythical half-lion, half-fish creature, is the official symbol of Singapore. An eight-metre-high, water-spouting rendition of the Merlion can be seen at the mouth to the Singapore River overlooking Marina Bay.

*t*he illuminating autumn lantern festival is best seen at the Chinese Garden in Jurong. But all around town, people hang chromatic paper lanterns in traditional Chinese designs or more modern formats like boats, fish and planes.